STARDUST AND BUTTERFLIES

Nathaniel Lews

stardust and butterflies

You may write me down in history with your bitter, twisted lines. You may trod me in the very dirt, but still, like dust, I'll rise.

Maya Angelou

nathaniel iews

CONTENTS

birth   6

growth   23

change   38

rise   48

Dear reader,

Stardust and Butterflies was a seed I planted since the beginning of lockdown in the UK when I was fourteen. Since I was young, poetry has been something that I loved, an art that has allowed me to claim my identity and connect with my emotions as a young person in today's world. This debut collection of poetry is a product of the poets who have influenced me in my journey, especially black poets, past and present, who continually inspire the progression of my work and expression.

Stardust and Butterflies is an ode to the teenager, a growing, awkward person with dreams trying to find their way in the world. It contains poems about self-love, image, growth, and all sorts of feelings across the imagined life cycle of a butterfly across four chapters. Each chapter is a crucial stage in this journey.

It has been a dream for years now for something like this to exist. This book has grown into something I am incredibly proud of creating, and I am so grateful that it is in your hands and that I can share this with you.

Nathaniel Iews

X

nathaniel iews

Copyright © 2021 Nathaniel Iews

Stardust and Butterflies

Perspective Press Global Ltd

All rights reserved.

ISBN: 978-1-914275-06-7

stardust and butterflies

birth

a flowering thing

picture me as a flower,
in bloom my petals rise
cut crystal in pastel pink
and spring colours, intimacy
between colour and shape
hypnotising in sunlight
it reaches to taste
the cotton candy cushions
of clouds up high, unmoving

van gogh painted
in simplicity and allure
picture me: a lotus flower,
young cherry blossom or rose
ornament to gaia's body

i rose from the earth
a child of celestial creation
my stem strong and firmly
rooted in the ground,
roots an unyielding tether
to my reality in bloom
like a daffodil sun
blowing into a violet horizon.

flow

and i will flow like water
twisting in cobalt blue and aquamarine
filling rooms with the vastness of my volume
replace your thirst with awe and curiosity
for the chemistry of the compound,
give you life and sustenance for free

and i will flow like water
free like pearly doves and palm trees,
water natural and mineral
crystal clear and collected fresh from mountains afar

and i will flow. like water
i will move so effortless
and fluid with time
flood and run over,
why flow when you can overflow too?

nathaniel iews

deep breaths

i have the credentials of a professional dancer,
freedom in the movements of my body
unrestrained and fuelled with passions' fire
hidden between the lush layers of afrobeat
and a bluetooth speaker, taking me on a trip
down eons and eras with beats in all the right places

thick and rich flavours of sound spur my hips
and i am a professional dancer,
a release of humour and giddiness
weaved into the waves of my arms
and performances every day in the kitchen,
living room and bedroom too, a house tour
that leave be breathless and whole with heat

and i will keep dancing
renowned, professional dancer and all
until it's time to retire
catch a few breaths
and take a seat.

stardust and butterflies

for the culture

you will find us in traditional attire
for a party on a sunday. well-dressed
and regal, as patterns hang from our bodies
in every colour like kaleidoscopic lights
mum fixing her gele for the third time
as she makes you take pictures from every angle.
you will find us dancing at a wedding
to 'no one like you' by p square
then davido up next, bodies trembling
to the beat in surrender as hips rotate like windmills
people blown off their feet from the heat
while aunties battle it out on the dancefloor.
in the corner you will find a child
with oily lips from fried plantain,
as if it were lip balm for a hungry mouth.
the cameraman will appear out of air
as thin as the non-existent quiet and take a picture
just as you were enjoying your jollof rice
and pretending to get drunk on a sparkling juice drink.
at the hair salon, you'll have your thoughts
and dreams braided into a single cornrow
feel the breeze blow against your skin fade
as the barber gives you a fresh shape-up.
we'll judge you from a distance
with the movement of our eyes

nathaniel iews

up and down, kissing teeth

giving your ear an electric shock, the residue
of irritation clinging to your eardrums
'face your books' is something you're told on a daily.
no one can take away your education
be a doctor, engineer, or lawyer so you can live a good life.
no one can take away your heritage
bathed in seasoning and ripened in sweetness,
head adorned with a heavy crown
a royalty that could never be imitated

beginnings

there is always a beginning.
fresh like linen sheets and lemongrass
new as sweet strangers you meet on the street
sparkling fervently in the glow of an indigo skyline
unknown to you, unmapped and unchartered
lands where riches are found in abundance:
gilded memories immortalised in frame
from a photo album you would pass down
from generation to generation,
becoming a wrinkled heirloom

these beginnings embody the joy of a birthday
when i can have mouthfuls of cake
victoria sponge in thick fondant
like saccharine wrapping paper,
they embody the anticipation of a new year
when i can compile resolutions
only to not change a thing.

beginnings birth chances for me to grow
into spaces, take up places
where i am meant to be. a genesis
where i can scribble my story in poetry and verse
cocooned in the golden light of dawn.

nathaniel iews

the morning

morning to evening
and morning again
in wake of water and sunshine.
repeating, and everything
has become second nature

waking up only to fall in love
so easily with sleep
and the solace of dreams,
the light comes to persuade again
and summon me from slumber

let the water fall, soak
into my roots and allow me to grow
into the morning and evening,
so vividly

when it rains

if only i could be like the rain
drip from floodgates beyond sight
a consuming waterfall,
blue velour hemmed in white whipped lines

i would pitter and patter on the earth
saturating the hair and skin
falling and falling, gracefully
and without permission or direction
like a prodigal son returning home

i want to embody its form,
soak the earth with a million
raindrops and let it sink in.
in impact, i'll make floods of me.

nathaniel iews

forbidden fruits

what is forbidden to me?
i wander through gardens of trees
empyreal and tempting in its fruits
hanging from branches as breakable as promises,
wild berries and apples as crisp as the crunch
of earth beneath naked feet
is mine to pluck and pick,
devour knowledge of my good
and bury the evil

i have heard of the temptation. i hear
the whispers of eden and her jewels,
fragmented in the rosy blush of apples
sweet and delicate as snow white was
in the wake of sleep and death

i could eat the fruit of my tree
it's not good to take apples from strangers
after all. i will water my garden
pick and pluck fruits from all trees,
none is forbidden to me.

this, that glitters is more than gold

a summer glow always comes
to devour and project the splendour
of this melanin, a mixture of gold
and the heavenly hues of blackness
and its majesty, an ancient royalty

the way it glistens in the sweltering heat
hypnotizing in its melody of skin
a safe to a multitude of riches within

edges of a body, a gold coast of tales
and endurance dripping in shea butter and cocoa too

this. an unconquerable continent
this. a treasure island of immeasurable wealth
this. a vessel steeped in gold
this that glitters and is more than gold.
golden and glowing, never leaving
the story of my creation untold.

lessons from children class

i was always told you reap what you sow
and so i sprinkled seeds into soil,
umber and hazel grains
where small seeds can lay to rest
sunflower seeds in the earth's arms
and cleansed in her anointed touch

i watered seeds small as mustard
with my glass tears that shattered
into pieces of will and want
i provided the light through my eyes
lighthouse and doorway to thoughts
of tomorrow's toil and sunrise

to germinate never came easy,
action or inaction
the consequences stayed the same,
a constant uncertainty.
these hands were never made
for gathering crops or planting seeds
i was never told that some seeds
i'd sown would never grow,
maybe my faith is smaller than a mustard seed.

ode to the vaseline in my pocket

tin of packaged reliance and cocoa butter
therapy to these lips
soothing to the shaky soul and skin
you placate the desert and droughts
an application of confidence
beyond the confines of this mouth
o entrance to speech and prophecy.

nathaniel iews

riffs and runs

play.
earphones in and sound on halfway volume
as sugared sounds of voice and instrument
pour into my ears like water pouring down a funnel,
it drowns these small eardrums of mine
coats it in an intro of instrumentals and echoes,
a harmony that hides calm in my eyes
unearths emotion in the keys and crescendos,
the riffs and runs of my mind, body, and soul

pause.
earphones out and sound still on
because i am worried that my music is too loud
and can be heard by others around:
it was only ever meant for my ears
i lower the volume, sacrifice sound
for comfortability, though the music
hits differently when it's loud, a flood of passion
that travels down my spine and inside
i am moonwalking on silk as smooth as sound
that blossoms clouds for me to rest on,
as if i am suspended in space or sky

rewind.
this part of the song didn't make me feel
like it used to, make me shiver or shed a tear
isn't that the power of rhythm n blues?

stardust and butterflies

to put you in the singer's shoes
whether it's a breakup or a make up
it's addictive, laced with a bit of sparkle and shine
and i am compelled to listen over and over again.
the cycle repeats, *press replay*.

mother tongue

what is more majestic than syllables
rolling off the tongue like a contained ocean wave
only to soak the ears with the sublimity of a sound
sweeter than the honeycomb,
leave the mouth with desire for the same love
to roll off it in the sacred art of intonation
and pronunciation.

pretty boy

you cloak yourself behind an illusion,
unknowable to everyone except you
pose for the cameras at day
close the curtains at night,
a fake thing fragmented into porcelain,
a shattered china doll. expression blank
like a poet's vacant sheet of paper,
cream secrets waiting to be unveiled

hide and seek for the dainty key
to a steel door, maximum security.
guarded by a sphinx armed with riddles
too intricate to solve and you are clouded,
blurry and unclear enigma bottled up in rhyme
afraid of strangers who stray shipwrecked
to your island, peek at your colours
then leave as pirates. you have been made
into an unpopular and unpopulated desert island.

who would honour your chrysalis,
just as much as your butterfly?
pretty boy.

nathaniel iews

growth

i shine, you shine

our light is a harmonious phenomenon
we shine together like synchronous morse code,
outdo stars and suns. floating orbs in a ghostly glow,
we coalesce from nebula to supernova
exploding in beguiling wisps of colour
illuminating every space we walk into

we have dreamt of sunshine, a golden tongue
ready to lap up our skin like an eager child
with chocolate and hazelnut ice cream in a summer heat
we dine as royals and eat the fruits of our love's labour
ripened passionfruit, tart, citrus and sweet

when noon falls, we won't wallow in the wind,
instead we'll walk on rainbows side by side
too bright and blinding for a night to exist
even in a december fog, we'll shine
as two streetlights, too bright
to get lost in the dark
when we have one another.

nathaniel iews

moonlight, camera, smile!

smile for me, luring thing
as i play an imitation game
with the crescent moon
lips stretching to a broad horizon,
a stage for performing arts
where sadness slips into
an impromptu vanishing act.

i wear my smile like cheap clothing:
simple plaid shirt and ocean blue jeans
to turn away prying eyes. you couldn't
unveil the language of these lips,
peel back the layers to uncover the truth
behind a two-faced smile

the double agent assigned to imitate
the twinkle of stars
conceal scars like plasters do,
waiting for healing and hoping to stay put,
forbid what's underneath to be revealed

if smiles won awards
mine would win best-supporting actress:
take a bow, exit stage
wash and rinse itself in tears
eyes a churning washing machine,

stardust and butterflies

for the same cheap clothing,
simple plaid shirt and ocean blue jeans
to turn away prying eyes by any means.

nathaniel iews

fatal flaw

imperfections run on a growing uncertainty
a body detached to its fleshly geography,
pinpricked in polka dot pattern, too out of style
to be seen as normal or a conventional tourist attraction
for unwanted attention and wandering eyes.
i would ask for a refund,
but i am with no receipt for return or renovation.
i could stand in front of a mirror forever,
fixed still-life portrait painted by light, reflecting
face in an illusion more desirable
than any selfie i have captured, yet
i am still trying. working to perfect
the art, the empty canvas of an empty vessel.
expert in reconstructing my image in my mind
like an architect with a collection of tools
my only tools are chemicals, whispering
packaged promises of purification and cleanliness
we meet in the morning and before bed,
a daily ritual. inscribing *spotless* and *glowing*
on my skin moving as pen on paper, still fragile
the mirror spells out my shortcomings from the mist
and i am compelled to repeat them out loud
and acknowledge its presence,
beautifully imperfect and flawed.

the binary of a tortured body

boy glances into mirrors
boy dissembles limbs like lego

there is no congruence to be found
only corporal dissonance

shapes dissimilar, shaping
a faulty vessel, fractured shell

boy disowns the body
dismembered and disjointed.

noughts and crosses

when i was younger,
i always played noughts and crosses
on my skin, fingernails like chalk
inscribing lines, x's, and o's
on the dark canvas of my thighs
what better games to play than with yourself?
to pass some time,
overshadow boredom with the feeling
of tickles and the hint of a smile
relinquish pixelated screens and synthesised music
for an intimate moment of alone time
where games become physical,
white drawings on my skin becoming a pastime.

a mundane experience

living forever sounds a bit bleak,
if only we could defy all odds
and stand firm against the storms of the weather

we would play songs from our youth
over and over, blasting bohemian rhapsody
as we slow dance in crowded fields.
it does sound a bit bohemian
the thrill of travel and mad ventures
migrating from stillness
to remote sands and seas

living in a cottage snuggled
between the trees is a must.
i need to fulfil my film driven fantasies
learn a new language, a tantalising tongue
to form a second identity:
so international and mysterious.

i'd create harmony from our breaths
make music of our lives that no one else
could have written for us and maybe
i'll become a holy man, question my sanity
and find peace. discover an equilibrium

nathaniel iews

between nature and humanity.

living forever sounds like any typical day
an unravelling of time, a show and tell
i would have no choice but to experience
replace the mundane with a life lived well.

music's spell

body swaying like palm trees
the music sets it on fire as though
stardust has been sprinkled on my skin,
euphoria takes control as my arms move
and twist to the beat, bad vibes have taken a seat

i'm in my own music video, glitter everywhere
plastered like tears to my face
i am without a single care
shoulders moving, bouncing up and down
body leaning in all directions. chest slowly rolling
like the wind coming to take your breath away
as my head tilts side to side in this sweet trance

purple lighting to set the tone,
a seductive ambience
topped with rimless purple sunglasses too.
sound is on max volume, rhythm n blues
slowed n reverb because it always hits different,
earphones in, echoes and sounds
moonwalking on aesthetic clouds.

nathaniel iews

3 am fake scenarios

fake scenarios and wishful thinking
are night-time hobbies of mine
that send me to sleep in elysian mists
of comfortability and the tranquillity
of twilight

and so tonight i don't have to drown
in tears for sleep to break the surface
but instead i can dream of fictional possibilities
that belongs in a celebrated novel
hidden on shelves in bookstores and libraries

i will surrender my wishes
and let them materialise
into warm blankets of my dreams
to be lulled into an abyss
where i can build a gothic library from the
bits and pieces of a paradoxical timeline.

half full and half empty

i am a glass half empty,
incomplete contents and unfilled to the brim
this frame of glass is fragile and delicate
as whom it represents, boy empty
on an unsatisfied bucket list
lost faces and patchy places,
one that has more to give
and more space to grow
into. for fullness to be poured in too
until i can rise and revel in feeling whole

i am a glass half full,
filled with the fantasies of a hopeless dreamer
stockpiled with sweet and salted popcorn
for the coming-of-age movie that is teenagerhood,
a peculiar experience for the books
where this fragmented existence resides
in broken glass pieces in their multicolour

and though i am not complete
i am full of what i hold
full of hope's helium
to float like a balloon,
a traveller on a distant highway

nathaniel iews

in the middle of nowhere
i will eventually get there, somewhere.

waiting to be multiplied in volume
increase until i am no longer confined
i am a glass half full, yet half empty
waiting patiently on a table
to be filled with something more
"can i get a refill, please?"

and he watches from my bedroom window

through the window, you glimpse me
weak and pellucid glass panes
a gateway to the lucid flow of your omniscient eyes
and carve me out in scripture,
holy one adorned
with the tear written letters
of yesterday night's prayers

i'm foraging for confetti-like miracles
i never managed to catch
with these tainted hands
and from the window
you roll the tape of a mundane reality
embedded in a messy room,
parisian artist portrayal of teen angst.
i am the pariah's showcase failing to pretend,
fear concealed things beyond shattered glass.

nathaniel iews

black tears

it was a divine night sky
dark like skin, the melanated
blanket upon my bones.

as i looked upon my face in the mirror
tears like glass pearls, salty melted stars
rolled down my cheeks over full lips,
plip plopping gently onto the island of my thighs.
what dull pearl or star could make my skin any more
treasured?

who would listen to the black boy's cries?
he cried because fear ate, him, whole
and convinced him, that one day his spirit too
from hatred's holy hands will go high
and be lifted, up, up in calm
far beyond the skies.

change

nathaniel iews

sending my condolences

please accept my sincere condolences,
i couldn't attend my funeral
watch from a distance in all-black
and sleek shades for dramatic effect
dressed in death's dark garments
as i dab crocodile tears with a white handkerchief,
tears the ground would be grateful to swallow
thirsty for sorrow to saturate its wrinkly surface

clutching my vintage pearls with gloved hands
i wouldn't want to be caught red-handed,
grey-handed from the ashes of things
i have set fire to with gasoline, invisible killer
sprinkled around generously like loose change
on the people i once was, once upon a time
i get money from the will anyways.

shadows and spirits trail behind me
blended into a grey cloak
twisting and writhing in agony,
murky mosaic of past selves:
the boy who always danced
listened to the radio after school
and hated vegetables

i hold funerals on a daily
final send-offs to closed chapters

stardust and butterflies

my pupil is a catacomb for the coffins,
dark and dreary depths where faces flash
in an optical slideshow, and it is me who will be
the only one in attendance.

nathaniel iews

starlight

heavy-eyed on dreams as soft as cotton pillows
i lay to rest in the solace of flowering fields,
the night sky dripping its ink into my eyes
an inkpot to contain the moon's iridescent elixir
leaking into the endless canvas of the sky

i have been practicing my calligraphy with the stars
hugging the cracks of moonlight
through the fiddle of my fingers, limbs loosely
scattered like the stars in its freckles against
the ripples of the dark, avant-garde artwork
in a night-time gallery everyone can witness

i'll fall asleep to my metronome heartbeat
moonwashed and laid down, hands behind head
my back tickled by greener grass, the cold wind
a wet tongue against my skin. calmed into bliss
the fresh fragrances of earth will greet me,
her lavender and roses

my mind, weightless
drifts off with the breeze
i have fallen in love with life again,
once more.

sour

it's bittersweet how your smiles
are never meant for me,
a mixed drink with sweetness's banal blend
but tinged with sadness's glacial residue
and i guess i am jealous,
maniacal tyrant of dead hopes
and expectations higher than
the 50 pence i owe you
living precariously
through slow burn fiction
and heart wrenching tv-shows
like a lovechild of romeo and byron
a delusional and hopeless romantic is i,
misreading attention
as some dose of affection
when it's just a drop of lime

nathaniel iews

crush culture

this feeling is known all too well
drowning, drowning in an ocean
of butterflies that buzz incessantly,
wishing that was your phone instead
you won't be getting that text or call

love-struck or lovesick, i'll be in need
of a box of tissues to dry honeysuckle tears
replace romance with reality, served stark
and i am drowning still, without recognition still:
a buoyancy aid to keep me afloat
so i can wash ashore on some beach as a seashell
that you hold to your ear, listen attentively
to my ocean-like love song
with a backing track the waves wove for you

gazing into your eyes resembles staring at the sea
something to sink in, surrender to salty depths
that leave me thirsty for a glass of water
but this isn't the movies, full of clichés
and the tired romance trope.
set the scene to me swimming ashore
to bathe in sun-kissed sands, lay alone
warmed by a tangerine sun.

honeyed whispers

the talk of your mouth always ends with me,
easily flowing fountain from your lips
like honey from a broken tap, corroded faucet
in need of manual repairs for a running mouth,
a prancing mouth dripping and dropping
in the secrets i whispered to you
regurgitated as viscous glitter, mass-produced

it's me in the mason jar,
packaged sample on sale sold cheap
for fleeting pleasure, fleeting laughter
dead as petals falling to land on eager ears,
you yearn to open the puzzle box
a challenge to tease your tongue,
test the waters to tell tales
trapped in a web of lies

i've never considered myself to be much of a spectacle
to you, i must be an addictive chemical
a cataclysmic catalyst to your guilty pleasure
and i wonder how long you could live
without my name being the period to your sentence.

nathaniel iews

rom-com

head over heels, i'm falling
into a bottomless well of feels
it's the typical cliché, the one in the movies.
giddy on unrealistic longing, you dream
from a distance so smitten with the idea

it's just a fantasy, rash and naïve
to think that you'll have your happy ending
boombox above head in a declaration of love,
unashamedly public
or even a serenade from your window,
how innovative and romantic!

cue swelling music,
locking lips in the rain as it soaks
through your clothes is a distant height
for an unconventional, twenty-first century
petrarchan lover

if romance was dead i would be immortal
nothing would be able to take my breath away,
anymore

comme des garçons

i don't want to be comme des garçons
follow the wandering herd
an emotionless machine crafted
from unoriginal components,
carbon copy to the thousands
hardened by unwritten rules
from blood and sweat
but no tears. tears as blue
as pink and still salty the same
wear a frown weaved from glass thread,
a flamboyant fragility.
i can't pretend to be somebody
you are not, the burly boy
made of artificial scrap steel
sporting a mask to conceal,
apply cheap concealer
to maintain the illusion.

nathaniel iews

here is what i remember

clear smiles that pained my cheeks
and the trace of a little boy's joy that lasted weeks,
a six-year-old walking down imaginary runways
in their bedroom and mum's high heels
indulged in the sweet caramel of my feels,
i wonder now, how with practice
i could have been a full-time model
in some other reality.

i reminder dancing with a quiet passion
like the mesmerising movement of flames
in the burning furnace of my soul
and i felt whole in that fresh feeling of liberty
from the tickle and touch on my bare soles

and how could i not remember
reading fiction into the night
with the partnership of poor sight
and a small flashlight

here's to remembering what it feels like
to not give a single care and feeling as though
i was the (l)on(e)ly one in the world.

stardust and butterflies

rise

the butterfly with broken wings

butterflies were created to fly,
spread their wings so all can see their scales,
iridescent stained-glass windows
consecrated in multi-colour,
o spirited monarch
a delicate heart beating
against the currents and gale.
behold the colourful creature, the collectors' prize
a flower fluttering and twirling in the gentle breeze
its blades rise, broken yet its body sings its artistry.
in being broken it has become a token
to the chapters of its story
a symbol of change and its life's range.
the butterfly is as light as a feather
we say it's fragile but forget it's agile too,
its wings gaily pigmented
an optical illusion of colour
reflective scales, its chrysalis once a corpse cover
i behold, the butterfly with broken wings.

dreamscape

serenity looks like a sunrise
lucid and golden,
blooming and glowing
it calls our names, a sweet lullaby
lulling and enticing with the taste of home.
i heard it sits near a rainbow, a utopia more tempting
than the vision boards we collate in our minds
a dreamscape sun-kissed, a dreamscape abundant.
there is no pretence here,
here we are not compelled
to conform or imitate the crowd
here we abide in the wrinkles of time and reality
untouched by judgment and fear
to be anything less than ourselves
here the only taste is sweetness on our lips
the only sight the sun rising
in a place warm and engaging
far away and in a distant location
at the genesis of dawn
and at the revelation of dusk,
a place we can call our own.

nathaniel iews

i want you around

you are a presence that defies magnetism
these wondering eyes of mine attract to you
but i am never seen by yours,
i guess opposites do attract after all
and i will never get the chance
to laugh in harmony with you
create an eternal symphony from the synchrony
of our heartbeats in closeness, feel
the softness of skin and milky balm of moon
someplace in a pretty flower field
a getaway of sorts someplace with someone
where i am wanted.

i don't know why i like you

engulfed by the bustling butterflies in my stomach,
i try to abandon the idea of you
discarded waste in denial's litter bin
and still find you here,
fluttery sensation in a confined burst
perplexing and trivial dreamboat
looking for something finer
softer than just anyone. simply not me
you have left me restless

look as you kindle the phenomenon with you,
as some divine apollo or adonis
from the glittering monarchs, the swallowtails
you won't notice me until i talk

awkward talk drowned in abrupt laughs
soaked from unknown chemicals and dopamine
an unknown thing.
maybe you are a ceramic figment of my mind
and you that's in the constellations,
it's you that's written in the stars

you're a memento of a bolted heart
organic kernel far behind a solid shell,
a shell which echoes effusively.
i'm too hidden behind brick walls

nathaniel iews

for me to be noticed, gifted
with a slight glimpse
or for your echoes to bounce off me

when we speak (you talk and i nod,
like a mindless bobble head)
— i collect your words like spare pennies
and the only thing my ears hear
is you asking me to run away with you,
we are two daredevil fugitives searching,
searching for a watercolour horizon.
i earth, you sun
because you belong in my orbit
so how can i look at you,
how can i look at you and not ask myself why,
i like you.

social butterfly

walking into a room is a death sentence
uncertainty sunk into the way i behave
calculated in precision and performance
as if i am on a runway, amateur model
layered in milky pearls and clown couture
waiting to trip from stiletto heels
encrusted in plastic diamonds clicking and clacking
an outdated soundtrack that no one listens to.

newton never discovered a law to my motion,
manufactured and mechanical movements
interwoven into my self-consciousness
and the cherub on my soldier tells me
to let loose, throw caution to the wind

like an apple falling from a tree
gravity will pull me, centre me in earth
take away all discomfort and unease,
what a blessing it would be to be socially dynamic.

nathaniel iews

strange folk

we are found balancing on the middle
of a tightrope, angelic acrobats
with hands locked together
like a key to a door, treading
on the lines of our elysian dreams
blotted out in the cloud and mist
of interpretation and judgement

we ask ourselves what it would feel like
to be pure and perfect
cherrypicked and chosen
as a strange apple from a tree

we cry, embrace, and laugh
as we recite the verses of a love
never written in black and white,
write sonnets and songs of an innocent desire
that is no test of sanctity or trial
we have walked farther than a mile,
passed thorns of guilt
and stopped bowing our heads
to ask why, only to meet somewhere
in the middle of a tightrope
suspended in teal and sapphire swashes of sky.

they say that when we fall
we'll fall to flames

stardust and butterflies

instead, we'll call each other by our names
and ascend.

nathaniel iews

labels

there seems to be an uncanny obsession with labels,
golden star stickers and fancy lettering to name you
capture your essence in a word, short and sweet
put yourself in boxes like a pair of new shoes
you'll shove under your bed. it's suffocating
to live behind four walls, packaged and marketed
as a keepsake that belongs in unfamiliar hands
to be inspected closely by clammy fingers
eager to mould your soul
in foreign fabrics, bargain and faux
it can only go skin deep
superficial tags that can melt into skin
and leave the inside untouched,
they can only etch the surface.

if i had a label
i would exist in the bakery section at tesco's
a pastry too fresh to be boxed up
a thing short-lived but sweet, nonetheless.

buttercream

faint kitchen scents tickle my nose
self-raising flour sprinkling across the countertop
in a shower of confetti (i'm not the best with sifts).
dad shouts over the sound of the cake mixer
that i shouldn't make a mess
but i'm messy anyways
chocolate chips melting at room temperature
cocoa power and caster sugar coating spoons
in butter-streaked bowls. it's a solo bakeoff
and i'm being a bit too generous with the measurements
the sweeter the better, right?
the oven thrums like a rumbling stomach,
anticipating a baked delight.

stillness

"don't be afraid," he says
from the static, the white noise.
a silent crook, stillness came to swindle
and steal time in its pocket watch
taking energy like debt,
rooting us to the ground as human trees
slow and stagnant runners
afraid of losing the race

how daunting it is to be still,
succumb to emptiness and silence
a boundless void punctuated in nothingness
screaming to be stuffed with noise.
something, anything

the silence beckons me to listen to its sonnets
dizzy and drowning in empty noise,
the pocket watch tells me
it is time to tune in.

a time where we can exist

turn forward time,
vintage grandfather clock
of oak and cherry hardwood
to where we first meet in a crowd
blotted paint against an empty canvas

you woo me, with your words
as soft as mulberry silk
and as rich as the ocean sunset
of your clear quartz eyes

and you tell me your story
not one for bookshelves or to be hidden in libraries
instead for these lonely and little ears
but in all honesty,
i'd prefer you tell me the specifics
of when you were born to make a birth chart,
uncover our compatibility

tipsy on the half-moon of your smile
i would smile too and laugh, sappy and stupid
until my cheeks ache
in the ruby blush of an apple
(if only you could see it)
i will know that you are a substance
to take with measured caution.

nathaniel iews

we would lie in a vast field
framed by pink clouds and indigo sky
a storybook setting of sunlight and shadow
on a picnic blanket of geometric print and pattern
the way it is in the movies
we'd drink cheap lemonade from plastic cups,
pretending to be anything more
than normal people.

bloom

in bloom
these petals extend, timid
like the body of a ballet dancer
twisting to a graceful rnb love song
a gradual unveiling
marked in coral shades and honeydew

encircled by light's touch
i will bloom the way popcorn does
a surprise bouquet of gold
and antique white blooms,
remember the small and light-hearted child
who was afraid of becoming, unfold
the corners of the page
and enter the next chapter.

watch as i showcase the pastel colours
pretty matisse flower composition
evolving with hope, blossoming
with the freshness of youth
a white rosebud opening-up
in the morning. you will find me
in bloom, in my own pace and season,
scorching sun or restless rain.

About the Author

Of Nigerian heritage and born in Ireland, Nathaniel Iews is an emerging young poet and writer from England. At the age of 15, he has already been published in anthologies and has been highly commended in the 2018 *Essex Poetry Festival Young Poet of the Year* competition. When not writing, Nathaniel can be found reading YA fiction or listening to music.

Stardust and Butterflies is his debut collection of poetry in which he explores the arduous journey of growth as a teenager through the imagined life cycle of a butterfly.

He can be found on Instagram @n.i.poetry.

About the Publisher

Perspective Press Global is an independent publishing firm representing authors under the age of 20. Our mission is to unlock the world of publishing for the next generation and remind them that there is no such thing as being 'too young.'

Perspective Press Global was founded by Eleni Sophia when she was just 18. Having been rejected from publishers as a teenager, Eleni Sophia recognised the need for creative outlets for young writers; she now works alongside young authors to help them get their voices heard.

Keep up to date with Perspective Press Global's latest signed talent and publications over on Instagram at @PerspectivePressGlobal

nathaniel iews

Copyright © 2021 Nathaniel Iews

Stardust and Butterflies

Perspective Press Global Ltd

All rights reserved.

ISBN: 978-1-914275-06-7

www.ingramcontent.com/pod-product-compliance
Lightning Source LLC
Chambersburg PA
CBHW021452080526
44588CB00009B/808